Getting To Know...

Nature's Children

CHIPMUNKS

Merebeth Switzer

Grolier

Facts in Brief

Classification of North American chipmunks

    Class: *Mammalia* (mammals)

    Order: *Rodentia* (rodent)

    Family: *Sciuridae* (squirrel family)

    Genus: *Tamias* (eastern); *Eutamias* (western)

    Species: *Tamias striatus* (Eastern Chipmunk); 16 species of western chipmunks

World distribution.   North American species exclusive to North America; closely related species (*Eutamias sibiricus*) found in regions of the Far East.

Habitat.   Mainly woods and forest.

Distinctive physical characteristics.   Five dark stripes on back; stripes on face.

Habits.   Primarily solitary; active by day; builds underground burrows; gathers and stores food; hibernates.

Diet.   Buds, seeds, berries, nuts, occasionally insects and caterpillars.

Edited by: Elizabeth Grace Zuraw
Design/Photo Editor: Nancy Norton
Photo Rights: Ivy Images

ISBN: 0-7172-8487-5

Have you ever wondered . . .

Chipmunks are one of nature's cutest animals. On summer days, they can be seen scampering about, their striped cheeks bulging with seeds. And when a chipmunk finds a special treat, it chatters with excitement.

But, friendly as they seem, chipmunks are secretive little animals. It's not likely that you will stumble across their home or ever see a baby chipmunk.

Why do chipmunks seem to be everywhere, yet at other times nowhere in sight? Let's look closer at this delightful little animal and find out.

A Word of Caution

Never feed or allow a wild chipmunk to get close to you. Some chipmunks carry *rabies,* a disease that is passed on to people through bites from infected animals. If you ever are bitten by a chipmunk, tell an adult immediately.

Where They Live

Most chipmunks live in forests and woods, but some are found at the edge of deserts and high up in the mountains. These places are very different from one another, but they have one important feature in common. In all of them, chipmunks can find hiding places and the low bushes and plants they need for food.

Chipmunks are ground animals, and all of them spend some part of their life in underground homes called *burrows*. So it is important that they live where the soil is dry and easy to dig. You'll rarely find chipmunks in swampy areas or in places with heavy clay soil.

Usually chipmunks do not live in towns and cities. If you do meet a chipmunk in or near the city, it will probably be living in an abandoned barn or house on the outskirts of town.

Chipmunks are found across much of North America. Notice, however, that there are none on the northern tundra, on the Great Plains, or in the hot, swampy regions of the South.

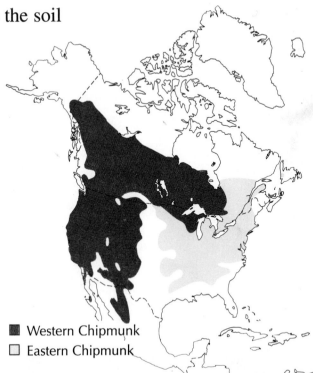

■ Western Chipmunk
□ Eastern Chipmunk

Dry, loose soil that's easy to dig makes homebuilding easy for a chipmunk.

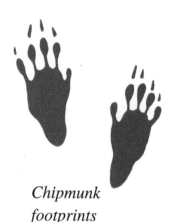

*Chipmunk
footprints*

Chipmunks Up Close

We all know the chipmunk with its light brown fur, light underbelly, and striped back. If you count the stripes you will find that there are five dark brown stripes separated by four white or beige stripes.

In western regions you might mistake a close relative, the ground squirrel, for the chipmunk. But look closely—there is one easy-to-spot difference. Chipmunks have stripes on their faces as well as down their backs. Many ground squirrels have plain faces with stripes only on their backs. And if you're close enough to count, you'll find that squirrels have different numbers of stripes.

There are many varieties of chipmunks in North America. This means that chipmunks may look quite different depending on where they live.

Unlike squirrels, chipmunks have stripes on their cheeks and on their backs.

The Eastern Chipmunk is larger than the Western Chipmunk and has a shorter tail for its size. The smaller western chipmunks—there are 16 different kinds—are almost all lighter in color. They have longer tails for their size. Western chipmunks spend more time in trees than their eastern cousins, and their long tail probably helps them to balance more easily.

Keeping Clean

Just like you, the chipmunk has to keep itself clean. And just like you, it does this by taking a bath. But a chipmunk doesn't bathe in water. It takes its bath in dust.

That's right, in dust! The dust helps to clean dirt and extra oil from the chipmunk's fur. It also helps to remove fleas and other small *parasites*, animals that live off the bodies of other animals.

When eating, a chipmunk uses its tiny but nimble front paws like hands.

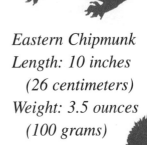

*Eastern Chipmunk
Length: 10 inches
    (26 centimeters)
Weight: 3.5 ounces
    (100 grams)*

*Western Chipmunk
Length: 7 inches
    (18 centimeters)
Weight: 1.8 ounces
    (50 grams)*

The chipmunk also cleans itself the way a cat does. It uses its tongue and paws to *groom*—brush and clean—itself. Grooming with the paws also helps to remove extra hairs from the chipmunk's coat. This is especially helpful for chipmunks in northern areas where they shed their coats twice a year.

Getting Around

Chipmunks never seem to walk—they scamper and scurry this way or that at top speed. They are good swimmers and even better climbers. So you need not worry if you see one dangling dangerously from a branch as it reaches for its favorite food. The chipmunk is one of nature's great acrobats, and it seldom loses its balance. If a chipmunk is being chased, it may even leap from one branch to another in order to escape.

Even the tip of a chipmunk's tail gets attention when this ever-active little animal grooms itself.

Despite their fast movements, chipmunks seldom go very far from home. In fact, they usually stay within about 160 feet (50 meters) or so of their burrow. This area is called their *territory,* the space animals live in and guard from intruders. If a chipmunk happens to wander into another chipmunk's territory, it will soon be chased out. Family members or a would-be mate are the only exceptions to a chipmunk's strict No Trespassing rule.

Chipmunk Homes

All chipmunks build underground burrows. Some live in them all year, others for only part of the year.

The pile of soil left behind when the chipmunk builds its burrow could be dangerous. It could show enemies where to find the opening to the *den,* as a wild animal's home or shelter is also called. Can you guess how the chipmunk solves this problem?

The tunnel leading to a chipmunk's burrow is only about two inches in diameter. That't just enough space for this wee animal to slink in and out.

It digs another entrance hole after all the work on the burrow is finished! It then fills the first *work hole* and uses only the new hole to enter and leave its den. For extra safety, the chipmunk chooses a sheltered place for this entrance, either in a brush heap, under a fallen log, or at the base of a tree.

Most burrows have a single tunnel that leads from the entrance to a den that sometimes is no larger than a coconut. Here the chipmunk makes a nest of shredded leaves, dried grasses, and fluffy seed heads. This nest will become a soft cushion for new babies or a warm bed in which to spend the winter.

Except for a mother with her babies, chipmunks live alone. Each adult chipmunk has its own burrow.

Fancy Homes and Plain Ones

The Eastern Chipmunk has only one home. It uses its underground burrow year-round and may live in the same one for several years.

But just like people who add new rooms to change their homes, the Eastern Chipmunk often adds new tunnels and rooms. This can create quite a maze of underground passages. The chipmunk may fill in old entrance holes or it may leave them open as emergency escape routes.

Desert-dwelling Western Chipmunks also live year-round in burrows. Other Western Chipmunks, however, use both an underground burrow and a high-rise nest in a nearby tree. They use the burrow as a winter home or as a

The entrance tunnel to a chipmunk's burrow slopes gradually. The den itself is usually about 1 foot (30 centimeters) deep.

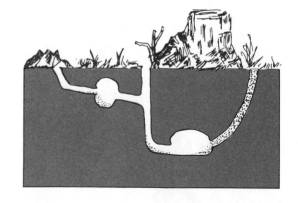

Eastern Chipmunks often add extra dens and tunnels to their burrow. Notice how the entrances are placed at the base of trees and rocks where they are less likely to be seen.

nesting place for the mother and her babies. Unlike the Eastern Chipmunk, Western Chipmunks usually build a new burrow every year.

The tree nest is a summer home for adults or for growing youngsters. Made of leaves and grasses, the nest is shaped like a ball and looks like a covered bird's nest. Some chipmunks may even take over a deserted woodpecker's hole for the summer. Chipmunks move into their tree nests when their burrows become too dirty or when their dens become infested with fleas or other parasites.

Most Western Chipmunks build tree nests which they use in the summer.

Chipmunk Chatter

It is sometimes hard to find even the noisiest chipmunk in the woods because its voice seems to come from different places. But look closely. A chipmunk twitches its tail in time to its call. This often gives away its hiding spot.

You can often tell what a chipmunk is feeling by listening to the sounds it makes. For instance, it sometimes shows pleasure by making soft noises deep in its throat or by chattering excitedly. When threatened, a chipmunk often chirps loudly, or scolds with a loud, noisy call. Chipmunks have many ways of showing their feelings.

Opposite page: *For such a small and charming animal, a chipmunk can look surprisingly fierce when scolding an intruder.*

Chipmunks live alone, but if two chipmunks meet they sniff each other's face as a greeting. They are able to recognize brothers and sisters by smell.

If a chipmunk sees danger, it runs away quickly with its tail in the air. Sometimes the chipmunk will make a loud chirping call as it runs, but often it will be silent, putting all its energy into running.

The chipmunk scolds an enemy or intruders from the safety of a tree. During this loud, noisy chatter, the chipmunk's tail bobs up and down to help make the point perfectly clear!

When a chipmunk is not sure if danger threatens, it sits up very tensely on its hind legs. It stamps one foot and then the other as it watches.

A Dangerous Life

Like many small animals, the chipmunk is important to the balance of nature. It is part of the diet of predators such as coyotes, hawks, weasels, snakes, bobcats, and raccoons. *Predators* are animals that hunt other animals for food.

You might think that the tiny chipmunk stands little chance against such animals. But the chipmunk is clever. It hides from predators by staying near plants or fallen logs that give it cover. If a chipmunk does find itself in danger, it quickly dashes up a tree or scurries into its burrow.

The chipmunk may avoid most enemies this way, but these tactics don't work so well with the weasel. The speedy and sleek weasel can catch a running chipmunk and sometimes even get into its burrow. The weasel is also an excellent climber and can follow a chipmunk up into trees.

Those lucky chipmunks that manage to keep out of the way of enemies may live as long as seven years.

Dinnertime

The types of food a chipmunk eats depends on where it lives and the types of food it can find. As a rule, chipmunks eat mainly plants.

Summer, therefore, is the time when there is a plentiful diet. Chipmunks can choose dinner from a variety of fruits and nuts. Their favorite foods include strawberries, blueberries, chokecherries, raspberries, wild grasses, and pine seeds.

But some chipmunks live in places where these plants are hard to find. As a result, they must look for other types of food. They may eat wild mushrooms, the roots of certain plants, and bird eggs. Some will even chomp on a grasshopper, beetle, or caterpillar. None of us can have our favorite foods all the time, and neither can a chipmunk. Any chipmunk will eat many of these other foods when it cannot find seeds and berries.

A chipmunk diet includes fruit, nuts, berries, seeds, and the soft parts of plants.

Whenever possible, the chipmunk carries its meal up onto a rock or tree stump, or to some other high spot. There it can keep an eye out for danger while it eats.

Unlike you, chipmunks don't need to drink water every day. They get most of their water from the plants they eat. Think of how much water there is in a nice juicy strawberry! Not needing a drink every day is especially important to chipmunks living on the edge of deserts and in other dry areas.

Spring is a tricky time for the chipmunk. By then, a chipmunk has eaten the winter store of food hidden in its burrow. But plants are only beginning to grow. At this time, a chipmunk will eat any food it can find—new sprouts, tree buds, and any of last year's seeds or nuts still lying on the ground.

Perched on a tree stump while eating, the ever-alert chipmunk can keep a watch out for danger.

Gathering and Storing Food

Chipmunks spend most of their day collecting and storing food. They carry away their groceries in their specially built cheek pouches.

These pouches are not wet on the inside like your mouth. They are dry like your skin, so that the food does not get wet when the chipmunk carries it. A chipmunk's cheeks can stretch to carry an amazing number of seeds. One chipmunk was found to be carrying more than 3,700 blueberry seeds in its cheeks!

In the early summer, chipmunks hide food in many different places. They may simply cover their treasures with fallen leaves or they may dig small holes and bury them. Small seeds are stored in clumps while larger nuts are stored alone.

A chipmunk has keen eyesight and a good nose for finding food. It can easily sniff out

The cheeky creature shown here has a way to go before breaking any records. Eastern Chipmunks can stuff six chestnuts into their cheeks—three in each side. That may not seem like a lot, but each chestnut is about size of the chipmunk's whole HEAD!

buried food stores. But the chipmunk buries so much food that it may forget where some of it is. When this happens, the seeds may sprout, growing into plants or even trees. The chipmunk is one of nature's gardeners without even knowing it.

Occasionally animals such as squirrels and mice steal from a chipmunk's food store. But our little friend also takes food from the hiding places of other small animals. In the end, it probably all works out evenly.

Getting Ready for Winter

In late summer, chipmunks in Canada and the northern United States begin to store food in earnest for the long winter. They select seeds and nuts because these will keep well.

To get the seeds from fruits such as chokecherries, the chipmunk carefully strips off pieces of the flesh with its teeth. Then it carries away the seeds and leaves the fruit in a small pile. If you ever spot a mysterious little mound of fruit on a fallen log or rock, you'll have a clue to who might have been there!

31

The chipmunk keeps its winter store of food under its nest. That way, in mid-winter, the chipmunk never has to leave its burrow for a snack. And what a snack. One nest was found with more than 68,000 seeds stored under it!

Winter Slumber

Chipmunks need to avoid the harsh winter when it's cold outside and there's not much food to be found, anyway. They do this by *hibernating.*

When an animal goes into hibernation, it sleeps through most of the winter. Its body temperature drops, and its breathing and heart-beat are much slower. With its body working at a slower speed, a chipmunk does not need much energy to survive the winter.

It does need some energy, however. That's why the chipmunk has to work so hard in summer to store away a good supply of food. Many other hibernating animals put on extra fat in the warm months to help them make it through the winter. The chipmunk does not. It relies only on its store of food.

But, you may wonder, if the chipmunk hibernates, when does it eat? No one knows for sure. Some people think it goes into real hibernation only after it has eaten its whole supply of food. A likelier possibility is that it wakes up once in a while and eats some of the nuts and seeds it has stored under its nest. Then it goes back to sleep.

In either case, the chipmunk is much warmer snuggled in its cozy underground nest than it would be outside. The new coat of woolly fur that a chipmunk grows in late summer also helps keep it warm during its sleep.

Chipmunks hibernate for different lengths of time, depending on where they live. In Canada, chipmunks usually begin to hibernate in late October or early November and stay in their dens until April. In the United States, a chipmunk's hibernation time is shorter. The milder the winter, the shorter the period of hibernation. In the southern states, it may last only a few weeks. Or winter may be so mild

As summer ends, a chipmunk starts growing the new fur coat that will keep the animal cozy all winter long.

that there's no need to hibernate. In those regions, you'll see chipmunks year-round.

Striped Sunbathers

On a cold spring or fall day, you might see a chipmunk sunbathing. That's right! It spreads itself out on a warm rock and catches some of the sun's warmth.

But too much heat makes chipmunks uncomfortable, just as it does you. Don't expect to see any chipmunks at noon on a hot day. They'll be keeping cool in their underground burrows. As long as the weather remains hot, they come out only during the coolness of early morning and evening. Chipmunks don't seem to like heavy rain, either. Like most people, they scurry for shelter in a storm.

Provided the weather isn't too hot, chipmunks enjoy soaking up a bit of sun.

Starting a Family

In early spring, chipmunks *mate,* or come together to produce young. The males fight to decide who will father the young. Sometimes one of them is badly injured by bites. More often, the chipmunk who is losing accepts defeat and scampers off before getting seriously hurt. This fighting is important. It means that only the strongest and healthiest males father the young. This in turn ensures the healthiest possible offspring. After mating, the male leaves the female and lives alone.

The mother gives birth in her underground den about 30 days after mating. The *litter* usually consists of four to six tiny babies called *pups.* The pups, born without hair, are both deaf and blind. They weigh about one-ninth of an ounce (3 grams). That's less than the weight of a nickel!

Baby chipmunks snuggle together in their nest. Pups grow rapidly. By summer's end, these furry little folks will be full-grown adults.

Like all mothers, a chipmunk mother takes good care of her babies. She *nurses* them—gives them milk from her body—many times a day. And she'll fight any intruder that comes too near her burrow—including other chipmunks!

Growing Up

After ten days, faint downy hair covers the pups' bodies and their chipmunk stripes begin to show. The babies do not open their eyes or hear well until the end of their fourth week of life. By then, they also are beginning to learn to walk, stumbling over each other as they move around the den.

Eastern Chipmunk pups remain in their burrows, but Western Chipmunk babies often are moved to a tree nest in their fifth week. The new tree nest is roomier and cleaner than the old burrow, and it may also be safer from predators.

This youngster, barely old enough to start exploring the outside world, already knows how to keep a cautious eye out for danger.

The mother chipmunk moves the pups one by one to their new home. As she carries them by the skin of their belly, the babies curl into a tight bundle with their head and tail cuddled around her nose.

By six weeks the pups are looking more and more like their parents. Their stripes are quite definite and their tail is getting bushy. The mother is now able to leave them alone for several hours at a time while she searches for food. But she returns often throughout the day to let them nurse.

Soon the young chipmunks are able to leave the nest and explore. But they seldom stray very far from home.

On Their Own

About half an hour before sunset, a mother chipmunk and her young return to the nest area. This is the time to play. The mother joins her youngsters in play-fights, games of chase, and follow the leader. These games are not only fun, they are good training. The young chipmunks become more skilled at climbing

Opposite page:
Play is important for young chipmunks. Whether jumping, play-fighting, or running after one another, pups use play to develop the many skills they'll need later in life.

and running, and they learn how to escape quickly when being chased.

Bedtime is at sunset. The mother and her babies go into the burrow and sleep, cuddled together, until sunrise.

By late summer, the pups are ten weeks old. They will have tried many different foods and they no longer need milk from their mother. Now they're nearly as big as mom and are ready to leave the nest.

Like their parents, the young chipmunks must begin to gather food for the winter. They must also dig their own burrows. The next weeks will be very busy for them.

Because they have so much to do before winter, these young chipmunks will be the last to settle down for their long winter sleep.

When they wake up the next spring, they will be ready to begin their own families.

By autumn the new chipmunks are on their own and—like every other chipmunk— busy gathering food for the winter ahead.

Words To Know

Burrow   A hole dug in the ground by an animal for use as a home.

Den   Animal home.

Desert   Hot dry area with few plants or trees.

Groom   To brush or clean hair or fur.

Hibernation   Kind of heavy sleep that some animals take in the winter, during which their breathing and heart rate slow down, and their body temperature drops.

Litter   Young animals born together.

Mate   To come together to produce young.

Nurse   To drink milk from a mother's body.

Parasite   An animal, for example a flea, that lives off the living bodies of other animals.

Predator   Animal that hunts other animals for food.

Pup   Name for young of various animals, including chipmunks.

Rodent   Any of a group of animals with front teeth that are especially good for gnawing.

Swamp   Area where the ground stays wet and spongy most of the year.

Territory   Area that an animal or group of animals lives in and often defends from other animals of the same kind.

Tundra   Flat land in the Arctic where no trees grow.

Work hole   First tunnel dug by a chipmunk when it is making its burrow.

Quiet and watchful one moment, scampering and chattering the next, the appealing little chipmunk is truly a wildlife treasure.

Index

PHOTO CREDITS
Cover: Bill Ivy. **Interiors:** *Valan Photos:* Thomas Kitchin, 4, 27; Herman H. Giethoorn, 6; Wayne Lankinen, 20; Esther Schmidt, 24; Harold V. Green, 30; Pam Hickman, 35. /Tom & Pat Leeson, 9. /*Network Stock Photo File:* Harold R. Hungerford, 45. /Robert McCaw, 13, 45. /Bill Ivy, 14, 29. /Norman R. Lightfoot, 17, 46. /*Tom Stack & Associates:* Mary Clay, 33. /*Lowry Photo,* 36. /*Parks Canada:* T. W. Hall, 39. /V. Claerhout, 41. /*Hotshots:* J.D. Taylor, 42.

Getting To Know...

Nature's Children

BEAVERS

Elin Kelsey

Grolier

Facts in Brief

Classification of North American beavers

      Class: *Mammalia* (mammals)

      Order: *Rodentia* (rodents)

      Family: *Castoridae* (beaver family)

      Genus: *Castor*

      Species: *Castor canadensis*

World distribution.   North American species exclusive to North America; related species (*Castor fiber*) found in Europe and Asia.

Habitat.   Rivers, streams, lakes in wooded country.

Distinctive physical characteristics.   Flat, wide, scaly tail; webbed back paws; large orange-colored front teeth.

Habits.   Builds dams and lodges; lives in family group called *colony;* mates for life.

Diet.   Bark, twigs, leaves, roots, water plants.

Edited by: Elizabeth Grace Zuraw
Design/Photo Editor: Nancy Norton
Photo Rights: Ivy Images

———————————

Revised Edition ©1996 Grolier Enterprises, Inc.
Original material Copyright ©1993, 1995 Grolier Limited

ISBN: 0-7172-8488-3

Have you ever wondered . . .

When you think of beavers, the first thing that probably comes to mind is the expression "busy as a beaver." Since early times, people have thought of beavers as eager, hard workers. In fact, one Native American legend tells of the Great Spirit building the earth with the help of beavers. Such a job certainly would have been big enough to keep a lot of beavers very busy.

Of course, beavers didn't really help build the earth, but they can fell trees of all sizes and use them to make remarkable dams and homes. Let's find out more about the real "busy beavers."

Beavers are perhaps best known for their skill in cutting down trees. To do the job, these hard-working animals have a set of truly amazing teeth.

Beavers: Who and Where?

Most of the world's beavers live in Canada and the United States, but there are some beavers in Europe and Asia, too.

The beaver has no close relatives, but it does have distant cousins. You can recognize them by their teeth. All beavers have big, very sharp front teeth which they use for stripping bark from trees and cutting and gnawing the wood underneath. Squirrels, rats, and gophers have sharp front cutting teeth, too. Animals that have these special teeth are called *rodents*. The name comes from a word that means "to gnaw or chew"—which is just what all rodents love to do!

Beavers are found throughout most of North America.

A beaver spends a lot of time in water. Its rounded ears and small nostrils can close very tightly to keep water out when swimming.

7

Beavers Up Close

The sturdy beaver is the largest rodent in North America. Most adult beavers weigh 35 to 70 pounds (16 to 32 kilograms). In fact, if an average-sized eight-year-old child and a beaver sat on either end of a see-saw, their weights would about balance.

An Amazing Tail

There's no mistaking a beaver's wide, scaly tail. It looks like a pine cone that's been flattened by a steamroller! This amazing tail serves many purposes. A beaver steers itself through the water by shifting its tail from side to side. When towing a heavy log, the beaver moves its tail to balance the weight. A frightened beaver slaps its tail against the water with a loud *thwack!* The sound tells other beavers to dive for safety.

A Beautiful Coat

The beaver's coat may not be as remarkable as its tail, but it's much more beautiful. Soft and silky, it can range from golden brown to

With its tail raised straight up, this beaver is about to whack the water with a loud splash. The sound is a signal to other beavers that there's danger nearby.

rich, dark brown in color. More important—especially in winter's icy waters—the coat is also very warm.

Why is the beaver's coat so warm? Because it has two layers. The outer layer is made up of long shiny "guard" hairs. Underneath is a thick, wooly layer of shorter fur. Such a fine coat is worth taking good care of, and beavers do just that. They even have built-in combs for the purpose—two double claws on each hind foot. These claws can open and close like a pair of tiny pliers, and the beaver uses them to untangle its fur and to comb out twigs and dirt.

In addition, all beavers have a pair of glands near their tails where a special oil is produced. A beaver spreads this oil through its fur with its paws to help the fur repel water. Even after an hour of swimming, a beaver's body stays dry and cozy inside its waterproofed coat.

In the wintertime, keeping warm and dry is especially important to the beaver. This beaver is grooming—cleaning its fur—to get ready for the swim home.

Beaver paw prints

This waterproofing is important because beavers spend much of their time cutting and peeling branches underwater. Most animals would soon get waterlogged if they tried this, but beavers never do. Beavers also have furry lips that close behind their front teeth to keep the water out of their mouths while they work underwater.

Very near the glands that produce the oil is another set of glands, called *castors,* where castoreum is made. *Castoreum* is a strong-smelling oily substance that beavers use to mark their *territory,* the area where they live. The smell tells other beavers to stay away.

Seeing, Smelling, and Hearing

Beavers have very small ears and eyes. But their hearing is excellent, and they see quite well—at least in daylight. They find seeing in the dark just as hard as you do. Yet beavers do most of their work at night. Instead of relying on their eyesight, they use their sharp senses of smell and hearing to direct them and alert them to danger.

Front paw

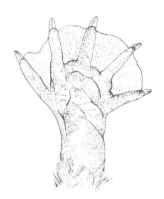

Back paw

Champions in the Water

With a flat tail for steering and strong, webbed back feet to supply the power, beavers are perfect water travelers. Their bodies are streamlined for swimming. Holding its tiny fists tight against its chest, a beaver glides through the water with only its head above the surface.

Beavers are also terrific underwater swimmers. Their large lungs can store lots of air. Most beavers can hold their breath for about ten minutes!

No matter what kind of fancy flips and dives a beaver makes, it is never bothered by water getting into its nose or ears. Beavers have special muscles that seal their nostrils and ears when they are diving.

A beaver's eyes are protected, too. Thanks to an extra pair of see-through eyelids that close over its eyes, a beaver can see just as well underwater as it can above.

The entrance to a beaver's home is carefully hidden underwater, but finding it is no problem for this animal. Beavers are expert divers and swimmers.

Clumsy on Land

Getting around on land is another story. Imagine playing tag in the woods while wearing swim fins! You'd trip all over your big, floppy feet and be easy to catch. Beavers have the same problem. With webbed back feet the size of ping-pong paddles, beavers are very slow and awkward on land.

For beavers, water means safety. When they go ashore to cut trees, they sniff the air and listen carefully to make sure the coast is clear of danger.

The more a beaver uses its teeth, the sharper they become.

Special Teeth for Special Food

A beaver's front teeth are quite special. Like your fingernails, these large teeth never stop growing! And a beaver must chew wood to trim its teeth just as you must clip your nails to keep them from getting too long.

A beaver's teeth may be strong, but they get an awesome workout. They cut trees, peel bark, gnaw branches, carry logs—and, of course, at dinnertime they chew bark and other beaver treats.

The outer surface of a beaver's front teeth has an incredibly strong orange coating. As the beaver chews through pieces of wood, the backs of the teeth wear down faster than the strong orange fronts. The more a beaver uses its teeth, the sharper they get for cutting.

The beaver's back *molars*, or grinding teeth, are special, too. They are as sharp and bumpy as a cheese grater. A beaver uses these teeth to grind up more than a pound (about 500 grams) of tree bark every day.

Special Food

You may prefer popcorn or ice cream, but tree bark is a beaver's favorite food. The beaver holds and turns a branch between its paws as it nibbles away at the tasty bark. Beavers do most of their feeding inside their homes or in the water where they are safest from *predators*, animals that hunt other animals for food.

When eating a twig or branch, a beaver looks a lot like someone enjoying corn on the cob.

In the spring and summer, beavers like to eat juicy shrubs and tree buds. During the fall, they eat more bark than usual, which helps them put on extra fat for the coming winter. They cut down many trees and gnaw them into short pieces. These are stored in big underwater piles near their homes. When the ice freezes over the top of their pond, the beavers have enough food stored underwater to last all winter.

It doesn't happen often, but if the winter is extremely cold, a pond may freeze all the way through. Unable to swim to their underwater food store, the beavers could die of hunger. But beavers are lucky. Their homes are built from the same thing they eat—tree branches. As long as the winter doesn't last too long, the beavers can survive by eating bits of their home!

When spring comes, a tender leaf is always good for a nibble. And it's probably a welcome relief from a steady winter diet of tree bark and branches!

Opposite page:

*A beaver usually
works alone when
cutting down a tree.*

The Beaver at Work

If you've ever had the painful experience of biting your tongue, you know how strong your chewing muscles are. A beaver's chewing muscles are much stronger than yours. With those powerful muscles and its very sharp teeth, a single beaver may cut down more than 200 trees a year!

When cutting, a beaver stands on its hind legs and leans back against its broad tail. It cuts with its head held sideways.

To fell a tree, a beaver bites the trunk to make a cut in it, then makes another cut farther down the trunk. But instead of chewing out neat slices of wood, a beaver takes several bites from the top cut and several bites from the bottom. Then it yanks out the wood that is left in the middle. The beaver's top teeth do most of the cutting while the bottom teeth help to steady its mouth.

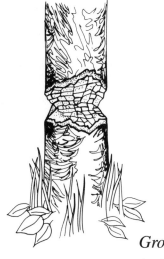

*Grooves left by a beaver's
teeth on a tree trunk look like
axe marks.*

Many people think that a beaver can make a tree fall whichever way it wants. It can't. In fact, it doesn't even know which way a tree it is cutting will fall. That's why a beaver cuts only until its teeth feel the last bits of wood just starting to break. Then—*whoosh!*—the beaver dashes for the safety of its pond.

The crash of a falling tree can be heard deep in the forest. Before leaving the pond, the beaver waits and sniffs the air to make sure the area is free of bears, cougars, or other predators out in search of a beaver lunch.

Getting It Home

When it's safe to go back to the felled tree, the beaver and its family begin cutting off the branches and dragging them back to their pond. If a log is too heavy for one beaver to carry in its mouth, two beavers work together, rolling the log along the ground with their front paws.

This is a small load for a beaver to haul. When a log is large and heavy, two beavers join forces to move it.

Once the trees near the pond are used up, beavers must travel farther from the pond to get trees. Sometimes when this happens, they dig canals that carry the pond water closer to the trees. Then they can simply float the heavy logs back home. Beavers have been known to dig canals as long as 700 feet (210 meters)!

Building the Dam

The perfect beaver pond is deep and surrounded by lots of trees. Beavers need to build their homes in deep ponds so that the underwater entrances are well covered. They also need deep water to be down far enough from the frozen pond top in winter. To make their ponds deep enough, beavers build *dams,* walls made to hold back water.

A dam works like the plug in your bathtub. The plug stops the tap water from running down

Beavers have teeth that never quit! The work in building dams such as this one is done mainly with a beaver's remarkable teeth and skillful front paws.

the drain. Beavers build dams across the low banks or creeks where water could flow out of their ponds. With these exits sealed, the water from incoming streams gets trapped in the pond, making it very deep.

Nature's Engineers

Beavers are born knowing how to build dams. They start their building by holding large sticks in their mouths and driving them straight into the river bottom. Almost anything that a beaver can find goes into the dam—wood, grass, rocks, and sometimes an old flashlight or boot!

A beaver dam is built like a layer cake. Just as the cake is held together by layers of icing, the dam is held together by layers of mud. Some people believe that beavers use their tails to hammer in branches and spread mud when building dams, but this is not true. Beavers use

To keep their pond's water where they want it, beavers must always be ready to repair their dams.

28

their paws and noses to smear the mud over their dam.

Beavers keep building their dam until they can no longer hear the sound of water running out of their pond. This sound is such an important signal for the beavers that scientists have been able to trick them into building dams by playing tape recordings of trickling water sounds!

Beaver Meadows

Some people get angry when a beaver dam floods a road or field. It's true that the dams can sometimes be a nuisance, but they can be useful, too—and not just to beavers! Beaver ponds become home to many new plants, fish, and animals.

Build-ups of solid material on the bottom of a pond can continue for years. This may eventually make the pond so shallow that the beavers leave. In time, a meadow—called a *beaver meadow*—replaces the pond.

This peaceful country meadow was once the busy headquarters of a beaver family.

A Home of Sticks and Mud

When the dam is finished, the beavers start building a home. There is a lot of variety in beaver homes—in fact, there are no two exactly alike.

If the beavers live in a deep pond, they may simply dig a *burrow,* or hole, in the side of the bank and live there. But if the banks are low, beavers build a special kind of home, called a *lodge,* in their pond.

The beavers start their lodge by anchoring sticks in the bottom of the pond and piling a huge mound of branches on top. With every member of the family helping, the mound soon reaches high above the water. The branches are cemented together with mud. Carrying the mud in their paws or under their chins, the beavers crawl as far up the slippery sides of the lodge as they can get. The mud that they dump flows down the sides, covering the lodge like syrup on a stack of pancakes.

Piles of sticks and branches lined up along a body of water are a sure sign that beavers aren't far away.

Because the beavers seldom climb all the way to the top of the lodge, that part gets very little mud. But a mudless roof is important. It allows plenty of fresh air to get into the lodge.

Making It Comfortable

When the outside of the lodge is almost finished, the beavers dive underwater and begin to chew a tunnel through to the center of the mound. They make a large living room above water level and then cut out at least one more entrance tunnel. The doorways to the tunnels are hidden underwater so that predators will not be able to get in.

Beavers will stay in the same pond and live in the same lodge as long as there are plenty of trees in the area. Like most homeowners, beavers spend a lot of time improving their homes. As the family grows, additions are built to make the lodge roomy enough for everyone.

When there's work to be done, the whole beaver family pitches in.

This is what you might see if you could slice off one side of a typical beaver lodge. Outside, the lodge looks like a pile of sticks. Inside, it's a comfortable home.

During the winter, the beaver family stays warm by snuggling together inside their home. Even when the temperature outside drops to -58°F (-50°C), the heat of the beavers' bodies keeps the inside of the lodge above the freezing point. A blanket of snow on the lodge helps trap heat inside, too.

When a beaver gets hungry in the winter, it takes a deep breath and swims out the tunnel to the underwater food pile that was made in the fall.

The Beaver Family

Cows live in herds and chickens live in flocks, but beavers live in a family group called a *colony*.

A mother and father beaver stay together for their whole lives. Though both parents help to raise the babies, it's the mother who makes the final decisions in a beaver colony.

Beaver parents, affectionate with each other, usually remain together their entire life.

Each year beavers *mate,* or come together to produce young, in late January or early February. During this breeding season, the beaver pair spends a lot of time frolicking and play-wrestling below the icy covering of their pond. The beavers mate during some of these playful underwater meetings.

A female beaver has to wait three and a half months for her babies to be born. While she is waiting, she prepares a special nursery inside the lodge. She builds warm, comfortable beds for her babies by splitting soft wood into thin chips.

A beaver mother likes to be alone when her babies are born. Shortly before they arrive, the father leaves the lodge and moves into a burrow at the edge of the pond. When the birth time comes, the mother beaver usually has four babies, called *kits.* As each kit is born, the mother carefully cleans its soft, fluffy fur. A newborn kit is about 15 inches (38 centimeters) long, including its tail.

Beaver kits are born with a tiny set of sharp front teeth, a thick furry coat, and a flat scaly tail.

Beaver Babies

Weighing a little more than a baseball, each newborn kit looks like a tiny copy of its parents. It even has a tiny set of sharp front teeth.

Beaver kits don't need swimming lessons. They can swim a few hours after they're born! Their thick fur coats trap so much air that the kits bob along the water surface like corks. In fact, the babies float so well that they can't dive until they've gained a few pounds! But since a floating kit would be an easy catch for a hungry hawk or otter, the mother keeps her babies inside the lodge for the first two months.

Just like new human babies, beaver kits wake up every few hours and cry to be fed. When they are *nursing*—drinking milk from their mother's body—the kits often sit on their mother's tail. Beaver milk is butter-yellow and as thick as toothpaste. This rich milk helps the babies grow quickly.

Opposite page:
A lodge makes a cozy home for newborn beavers. The kits use their tiny sharp teeth just a few days after birth. That's when the mother starts bringing tender young leaves for the kits to eat.

43

Opposite page:
*Beaver parents
teach their kits to
dive when they
hear a tail slap
against the water.*

A Lot To Learn

The kits learn many things by copying their parents and older brothers and sisters. When they see an older beaver chewing on a leaf, they rush over to have a taste. If another beaver dives for a branch, they dive, too.

One important lesson the kits must learn is how to recognize danger. They are taught to sniff the air for the smell of wolves, cougars, and bears and to watch and listen for otters, hawks, and owls.

Both beaver parents are quick to help a whining kit. They will often carry the kits from danger by holding them in their mouths or scooping them up in their arms.

Growing Up

Beaver youngsters live with their parents for two years. Because a new *litter*—a group of animals born together—arrives every year, a typical beaver family has about ten members—mother and father, one-year-olds (called *yearlings*), and kits.

The yearlings usually move out temporarily with their father when the new litter is to be

born. By this time, the yearlings are helping with the cutting and carrying chores, and with any repairs needed to the dam or lodge.

At two years of age, the young beavers are ready to leave home. They have to leave to make room for a new litter of kits. Most of them go willingly, but once in a while a straggler needs to be sent off with a hiss or a slap from mom or dad.

The young beavers may travel far before they settle down. Most, however, will pick a spot within 6 miles (10 kilometers) of their parents' pond. They soon find mates and set to work busily building dams and lodges for their own new colonies.

Words To Know

Beaver meadow   Meadow created when a beaver pond dries up.

Breeding season   The time of year during which animals mate.

Burrow   A hole dug in the ground by an animal for use as a home

Canal   A path or trough dug out for water to flow in.

Castoreum   Oily substance in a beaver's body produced by glands called castors.

Colony   A group of the same kind of animals living together.

Dam   A kind of wall built to hold back water.

Groom   To brush or clean hair or fur.

Guard hairs   Long coarse hairs that make up the outer layer of a beaver's or other animal's coat.

Kit   Name for the young of various animals, including the beaver.

Litter   Young animals born together.

Lodge   Beaver home built in the water, out of logs, sticks, and mud.

Mate   To come together to produce young.

Molars   Large back teeth used for grinding.

Nursing   Drinking milk from a mother's body.

Predator   Animal that hunts other animals for food.

Rodent   An animal that has front teeth especially adapted for gnawing.

Territory   Area that an animal or group of animals lives in and often defends from other animals of the same kind.

Webbed feet   Feet in which the toes are joined together by flaps of skin.

Yearling   Animal that is one year old.

Index

PHOTO CREDITS
Cover: Wayne Lankinen, *Valan Photos.* **Interiors:** *Valan Photos:* Dennis W. Schmidt, 4, 29; Wayne Lankinen, 6; J.A. Wilkinson, 19, 45. /Tom & Pat Leeson, 9, 16. /Norman R. Lightfoot, 10, 30, 33, 41. /Robert McCaw, 13. /*Hot Shots:* J.D. Taylor, 15; Steve McCutcheon, 25. /Bill Ivy, 20. /*Lowry Photo,* 23. /*NFB Phototèque,* 34. /*Tom Stack & Associates:* Gary Milburn, 26; Nancy Adams, 39; W. Perry Conway, 42.